STRATEGIC MANAGEMENT

DR. ABHISHEK VENKTESHWAR | SAVITHA NAGARAJ | DR. ASHA S &
BAISHAKI DEBNATH

ISBN 979-888521548-0

Dedicated to

My Mother- Dr.Abhishek Venkteshwar

My Husband-Savitha Nagaraj

My Family-Dr.Asha S

My Daughter- Baishaki Debnath

Contents

Foreword

ABOUT THE BOOK

This book provides practical advice on how to strategize in a concise way. It then guides the reader on how to formulate the strategies, review it , develop the framework, select a suitable research methodology, and analyze the results.

Preface

ABOUT THE BOOK

This book provides practical advice on how to strategize in a concise way. It then guides the reader on how to formulate the strategies, review it , develop the framework, select a suitable research methodology, and analyze the results.

Acknowledgements

This book has been a gratifying experience in the journey of our life. We thank God for his blessings in this endeavor.We would like to thank the President-Jain University trust and Chancellor Dr Chenraj Roychand, who has been our mentor and a guiding light. His words of wisdom have inspired us to write this book. We are also grateful to Dr Dinesh Nilkant, Director –JU-CMS for constantly supporting and encouraging us.We also take this opportunity to thank Dr N.Sundarrajan, Pro- Chancellor, Dr Raj Singh, Vice Chancellor, Prof. Sunitha B.K,HOD-JU-CMS, Dr Roopa Traisa, HOD-JU-CMS ,Dr Umankanth, HOD-JU-CMS, Prof Anila Bajpai, HOD-JU-CMS, Ms Jayashree and Ms Chaitra Shetty Coordinators- JU-CMS for constantly supporting us in this journey. We would also like to thank our family, friends, colleagues and students for motivating us to write this book.Finally, we are sincerely obliged to all those who have directly or indirectly helped us in the completion of this book.

Prologue

ABOUT THE AUTHORS

Dr. Abhishek Venkteshwar

Dr. Abhishek Venkteshwar is an Assistant Professor, Course Facilitator and Head-Student Council at Center for Management Studies, Jain (Deemed-to-be) University. He is the recipient of three gold medals for Academic excellence in PhD, M.Phil., MBA and B.Sc (Hons). He is UGC-K-SET qualified and certified in University Teaching by Harvard University, Yale University, IIM-Bengaluru and ISB-Hyderabad. Abhishek is a certified awarder in the 'Duke of Edinburgh International Awards'. He was also the Academic Coordinator (Entrepreneurship) at Babson College, USA from 2017-18. He has authored more than 45 papers in several UGC care / Scopus indexed International journals and over 12 books published by Amazon, Notion press, Eureka and Sapna Book House. Abhishek in a span of 8 years has won several awards for teaching and research. He was awarded the most coveted "Best Professor" (Under 30) in RULA International Awards (
2020), Global Leadership Awards (2019) and DR Research Awards (2018). In 2021, he was awarded an honorary doctorate from University of NJ for his contribution to research and teaching (under 30). He has been a part of several panel discussions on the Union Budget on various national television channels.

Savitha Nagaraj

Savitha Nagaraj is an Assistant Professor at Center for Management Studies, Jain (Deemed-to-be) University. She has a taught of wide range of subjects in the field of Business. She also developed and streamlined an innovative course tiled 'Entrepreneurship'.

Dr. Asha .S

Dr. Asha is an Assistant Professor, Course Facilitator, Coordinator-PCL and Head-Employee Engagement at Center for Management Studies, Jain (Deemed-to-be) University. She has a taught of wide range of subjects in the field of Human Resources. She also developed and streamlined an innovative course tiled 'Case Analysis'. She is UGC-NET qualified and certified by IIM-Bengaluru. She comes with a rich experience of a decade in academics and industry. Asha is a certified awarder in the 'Duke of Edinburgh International Awards' She has several papers in her kitty.

Baishaki Debnath

Baisakhi Debnath works as an Assistant Professor and Course Facilitator at CMS-Jain Deemed-to-be University, Bangalore. She has about a decade of experience in academics and possesses a keen interest in research. Her domain of interest includes People and Crisis Management, Organisational Behaviour and Organisational Change, Leadership, Employee Relations, Learning Organizations, Project Based Learning, Positive Psychology and Women Entrepreneurship.

CHAPTER ONE

Introduction to Strategy

Definition, meaning, relevance, characteristics, A Model of strategic management process, Approaches to strategic decisions making. Pitfalls in strategic management, Strategists and their roles in strategic management.

Introduction:

Strategy is a broad concept that covers a multitude of different issues, concepts, and methods. Many topics are considered in the formulation and implementation of strategy including industry analysis, competitors analysis, ethics, strengths/weakness, value creation, technology, innovation, product development, diversification, balancing the needs of various stakeholders, strategic alliance, organizations design, virtual organization, reward system, corporate cultures and corporate governance.

Every business organization of all sizes must prepare for an increasingly complex future, companies must deal with variety of strategic, technological and organizational forces on a daily bases. All these forces work together to redefine the economics and competitive landscape of the industry. Forward looking firms will seek to create new sources of competitive advantage by participating and shaping how industries evolve in the times ahead. Yet some challenges also threaten to erode the long held competitive advantage of companies that are slow to react or unable to mount an effective response.

For practicing managers and leaders, strategy is at the center of the effort to create value for customers, to respond to competitive challenge, and to build strong organizations.

Globalization has become etched in our competitive landscape, including new opportunities and threats from emerging and developing countries that are fast becoming vibrant competitors. Companies are continuing to innovate breakthrough products and services and technologies to serve customers at ever faster rates. They are planning and organizing their activities using new methods, techniques and modes of operations, especially with the pervasiveness of the Internet and the rise of 'virtual' ways of doing the things. They are reaching to new customers in new parts of the world they never previously entered.

Today all firms will necessarily compete with each other in the same way. Each firm is likely to devise its own strategy to deal with its competitive rivals to serve its particular base of customers, and to act on the changes that impact the way it operates. Each firm needs to develop a competitive advantage in its strategy that enables it to compete effectively.

Strategy refers to the ideas, plans, and support that forms employs to compete successfully against their rivals. Strategy is designed to help firm to gain an edge over its rivals which generates successful performance over an extended period.

Definition of strategy:

Harvard's Alfred Chandler" Strategy is a determination of the basic long term goals and objectives of an action and allocation of resources necessary for carrying out these goals"

James.B.Quinn "Strategy is a pattern or plan that integrates an organization's major goals,policies, action sequences into a cohesive whole."

William Gluick" Strategy is unified comprehensive and integrated plan designed to ensurethat the basic objective of the enterprise are achieved."

Henry Mintzberg" Strategy represents a fundamental congruence between externalopportunity and internal capacity. It is a pattern in a stream of decisions and action"

Features of a Strategy:

Strategy is course of action through which an organization relates itself with the environment so as to achieve pre-set goals.

1. Strategy links the organization to its environment.-Strategy relates the organization withits environment, to judge the feasibility of new products, to set objectives etc, environment and the firm influence each other in a systems approach, so it is very crucial to take changing environmental forces for the growth of the firm.

2. Strategy combines Factors like strength and weakness: A strategy is instrumental inrelating the organization to its environment, firm's strength and weakness. To capitalize on the opportunities, it must weigh first the threats associated with it and then its strengths and weakness. It has to be keen observer in each course of action.

2

3. Strategy is relative combination of actions.:A combination reached to meet a particularcondition or a situation to solve certain problems or to attain a desirable goal.

4. Strategy is forward looking: Business situations are changing in their entire dimensionmaking present situation obsolete, warranting new and creative approach to solve the problems that arises.

5. A strategy is complex and highly undependable for repetition. Gray Hamel has quoted the

'Yesterday's success will not guarantee today good performance, and today's success will not be help to be future leaders". Environment is highly volatile, strategies once implemented will not be usable again, their become cases to assessment.

Need/relevance for Strategy:

1. To have rules to guide the search for new opportunity both inside and outside the firm.

2. To take high quality project decisions.

3. To develop measures to judge opportunities.

4. To have an assurance that the firm's overall resources allocation pattern is efficient.

5. To have and develop internal ability to anticipate change.

6. To save time, money and executive talent.

7. To identify develop and exploit potential opportunities.
8. Improved integration.
9. Develop field of study by research.
10. Increase the probability of better performance.
11. To take systematized business decisions.
12. To improve communication and coordination in business.
13. Improves allocation of resources.
14. Helps the manager to have a holistic approach.

5P'sof strategy: Mintzberg has developed a useful framework for understanding strategy:

- **Plan:** intended course of action.
- **Purpose**: consistent stream of actions because of deliberate planning or emergent situations.
- **Play**: tactical play

3

- **Position**: location of the organization relative to competitors and other environmental factors.
- **Perspective**: personality of the organization

BUSINESS STRATEGY SHOULD:

Internal

External.
Internal
Strength
opportunity
Apply, sustain
Discover
Strategy
overcome
Avert.

Weakness

Threat

Forms of strategy: Henry Mintzberg a very influential management scholar at McGill University has identified different forms of strategy:

- **Intended strategy**: It is a corporate level strategy in which organizational decisions aredetermined only by analysis, for various reasons the intended strategy hardly survives in its original form. Unforeseen environmental developments, resource constraints, will result in some parts of the intended strategy being unrealized.

- **Deliberate strategy**: strategist will want to take advantage if new opportunity presented bythe environment even if it is not the part of intended strategy, they are secondary set of plans to support and maneuver the intentions. For eg, when government gave subsidies for solar power generations, many business have increased their investment and hiring in this sector.

- **Emergent strategy**: the complete new strategy or changes in the existing strategy because ofunforeseen events in the external environment can be termed as emergent strategy. For eg: to avoid the saturated markets in the cities for Flat TVs Toshiba concentrated to increase sales in rural markets of India.

- **Realized strategy**: strategy which organizational decisions are determined by both analysisand unforeseen environmental developments.

4

EMERGENT AND DELIBERATE STRATEGIES

Intended

Deliberate

Realized

Strategy

Strategy

Strategy

Unrealized

Emergent

Strategy

Strategy

Levels of Strategy: Strategy operation takes place at different levels namely, corporate, business and functional levels.

- **Corporate level strategy**: decisions making machinery consists of mainly members of BOD,CEOs, and administrative members. They are responsible for financial and non-financial performance of the organization on the whole.

  Their roles involve:

a. Defining the mission and goals of the organization.

b. Determining what business it should be in.

c. Allocating resources among different business areas.

d. Formulating strategies that span individual business.

e. Providing Leadership to the organization.

f. Corporate people are guardians of stock holder's welfare

- **Business level strategy:**These mangers are responsible to translate the general statements ofdirection and the intent generated at the corporate level into solid functional objectives and strategies for individuals business division or SBUs. These level strategies determine the basis on which a firm can compete in the selected product market filed. For eg: TATA's SBUs are

  Tata Steel, Tata motors, TCS, TCL etc.

- The role is:

  a. To translate general statement of direction for individual business.

  b. Design decision on which a firm can compete in the selected market.

  C) Concerned with strategies that is specific to a particular business.

5

°**Functional level strategy:**their basic responsibility lies in developing annual objectives andshort term strategies in the areas of production and operations research and developments, basically which is functional for fulfilling the corporate objectives. They also include the departmental functioning like HRM, Operations, Marketing, finance and accounting who are responsible for implementation or execution of company's strategic plans.

The roles they play are:

- Designing functional strategy in tune with business and corporate strategy.

- Provide information and feedback upwards to formulate realistic and attainable strategies.

- They are responsible for strategy implementation and execution of corporate strategy.

- In short, corporate level strategy occupies the highest level of strategic decisions making, which is more value oriented, conceptual. At business level, strategies are more comprehensive related to the business portfolio, of resource allocation and coordinating functional areas in SBU's and at the functional level are restricted plan accommodating objectives for specific function and coordinating different operations in achieving SBU's and corporate objectives.

Difference between Corporate, Business & Functional Strategy

Characteristics

Corporate

Business level

Functional level

level

Scope

Entire Org.

SBU or single

Functional Area

business co.

Source &

Board of directors/

Corporate strategy

SBU strategy

Motivation/Direction

CEO

Responsibility

Top level

Top level SBU

Functional level

corporate

managers or Top level

managers

managers

single business co.

managers

Time Horizon

Long term

Medium to long term

Short to long term

Specificity

General statements

Concrete &

Action &

of overall direction

Operationally oriented

implementation
& intent
oriented
Type
Conceptual
Mixed
Operational
Flexibility
High
Medium
Low
Cooperation
Considerable
Moderate
Little
Required
Cost
Major
Medium
Modest

6

Definition of Strategic Management:

- Strategic management is a process, directed by top management, to determine the fundamental aims or goals of the organization and ensure a range of decisions which will allow for the achievement of those aims in the long term, while providing for adoptive responses in the short term.
- Strategic Management is defined as the set of decisions and actions resulting in formation and implementation of strategies designed to achieve the objectives of an institutions---John and Richard.
- SM is a complex of strategic planning and implementation of strategies. –Prof. John Pearce.
- *Art & science of formulating, implementing, and evaluating, cross-functional decisions that enable an organization to achieve its objectives (David 2005)*

Features of Strategic management:

- Strategic decisions warrant top management support.
- Strategic issues involve allocation of large amount of resources.
- Strategic issues have a long term impact on the firm.
- They are future oriented.

- Strategic issues involve cross-functional and multi-layered managerial personnel.
- Strategic issues gives due weight age to the firm's external environment.
- Strategic management is a continuous process.
- Strategic management emphasizes on both efficiency and effectiveness.

Benefits of Strategic Management:

Benefits of strategic management can be divided in financial and non-financial benefits:

1. Strategic Management helps an organization to be pro-active in shaping future.
2. SM not only helps organization to respond to the environment, but also influence its environment by exerting control over its destiny.
3. SM helps organization to achieve understanding and commitment of all managers.
4. SM achieves participative management.

7

5. SM leads to long-run commitment to high performance of business.
6. SM enhances problem-prevention capabilities of the organization.
7. SM allows identification, prioritization and exploration of opportunities.
8. SM helps to integrate the behavior of individual into total effort.
9. SM encourages favorable attitude towards change.

Model of strategic management process:

Strategic management process is the steps, by which management converts a firm's values, mission, and goals/ objectives into a workable strategy,

It consists of Eight stages:

(2)
(3)
Identify
Analyze
the
the
Opportunites
(1)
environment

and threats

Identify
the
(6)
(7)
(8)
Org.'s
current
Formulate
Implement
Evalute
mission
strategies
strategies

result
and
strategies
(4)
(5)
Analyze
Identify
the
strengths
Org.'s
and
` resources
weaknesses

Strategic Management

21

Lakshman K

STRATEGIC MANAGEMENT PROCESS..

This process is most applicable to strategic management at the business unit level of the organization. For large corporation strategy at the corporate level is more concerned with managing a portfolio of business, involves strategy decisions about which business units to grow, resources allocation among the business units, taking advantage of synergies among the business units, and mergers and acquisitions

8

Step: 1 Establishing vision, mission and goals/objectives:

Vision statement: Is the likely status the firm wants to achieve in the long run. Vision statement sets the mood of where the company should go.

MISSION: A company's mission is its reason for being. The mission often is expressed in the form of a mission statement, which conveys a sense of purpose to employees and projects a company image to customers.

Task of the Mission statement:

1. Inject sense of purpose into firm's purpose.

2. Provide long term direction.

3. Give the firm an identity.

4. Decide' who we are', what we do', & where we are headed'.

Components of mission statement

(1)**Customers:** Who are the organization's customers?
For Amul : `Teenagers, Children
For Parle-G : all age group people
(2)**Products or services**
(3)**Markets:** Where does organization compete geographically?
E.G.---Amul emphasis is on whole india.

(4)**Technology**: Company should update with the technology with reference to the product and service they offer to customer to over come the competition.

(5)**Philosophy:** What are the organization's basic belief, values, and ethical priorities?

(6)**Self concept**: What are the organization's major competitive advantage and core competencies?

(7)**Concern for public image**: How responsive is organization to societal and environmental concern?

9

(8)**Concerns for employee**: Dose the organization consider employee a valuable asset?

(9)**Concern for survival growth and profitability**

OBJECTIVES:

Objectives are concrete goals that the organization seeks to reach, for example an earnings growth target.

The objective must be achievable and challenging, and measurable so that the company can monitor its progress and make corrections as needed.

Task of Objectives:

1. Convert mission into performance targets.
2. Create yardsticks to track performance.
3. Establish performance goals required for the task.
4. Push firm to be inventive, intentional, and focused. Eg: Strategic objective of the firm:

1. Increasing the firm's market share.
2. Overtake rivals on quality/customer service.
3. Attain lower overall costs.
4. Become leader in new product introduction.
5. Achieve technological superiority

This step address how organization must have clearly articulate goals and objectives in order to Channel the efforts of individuals throughout the organization towards common goals. Goals and Objectives also provide a means of allocating resources effectively. A firm's vision, mission, and strategic objectives form a hierarchy of goals that range from broad statements of intent and bases for competitive advantage to specific measurable strategic objectives.

Example:

10

- **Current Objective:**Reliance communication's current objective is to capture 30%Indianmarket share
- **Current strategies**: 50 paisa/min in all over India for **LIFE-TIME** just in Rs.48

Step 2 : SIUTATION ANALYSIS / ENVIRONMENTAL SCAN

Change in environment often presents new opportunity; an environment scan is performed to identify available opportunities. A firm must also know its internal strength and limitations to pursue the opportunity for viable success. The situation analysis involves both the external and internal scan.

The environmental scan includes the following components:

1. Internal analysis of the firm.
2. Analysis of the firm's industry (task environment)
3. External macro environment (PEST analysis)

Managers must scan and monitor the environment as well as analyze competitors. Such information is critical; in determining the opportunity and threats in the external environment.

The internal analysis can identify the firm's strength and weakness and the external analysis reveals

Opportunities and threats. An industry analysis can be performed using a frameworkdeveloped by Michael Porter known as Porter's Five Forces. A situation analysis can generate a large amount of information, which can be selective managed to create a model of SWOT analysis.

STEP:-3 IDENTIFYING OPPORTUNITIES AND THREATS:

- **OPPORTUNITIES:**- Positive trends in external environmental factors
- **THREATS:**- Negative trends in external environmental factors

11

Example: ICICI Bank

Opportunities

Rural financing and loans to small enterprises could increase the market share and profitability of ICICI Growth in general insurance industry will help increasing the market share of ICICI Lombard General Insurance Company

Threats

Opening of Indian banking sector in 2009 would cause intense competition

Global and domestic economic slow down could affect financial performance of ICICI

STEP-4: Analyzing the organization's resources and capabilities

- Skills and abilities of employee
- Available resources
- Financial position

- Quality of it's product and services

Example:- Amul

Every day Amul collects **<u>7 million litres</u>** of milk from 2.6 million farmers (many illiterate), converts the milk into branded, packaged products, and delivers goods to over 500,000 retail outlets across the country

<u>Step 5 – Identify strength and weakness</u>

- **<u>Strengths:-</u>**Any activity the organisation does well or any unique resources that it has.

- **<u>Weaknesses:-</u>**Activity the organisation does not do well or any resources It needs but doesnot posses

• **<u>Example</u>: Pepsi**

- **<u>Strength</u>**

12

  - Pepsi has a <u>broader product line</u> and outstanding <u>reputation.</u>
    - Increasing market share and revenues.
    - Availability of large free cash flow

- Great brands, strong distribution, innovative capabilities

- **<u>Weakness</u>**

(1)PepsiCo is far away from leader Coca-cola in the international market - demand is highly elastic.
(2) Pepsi had to inspire vision and direction for large global company.
(3)Not all PepsiCo products bear the company name

<u>Step 6: Strategy Formulation.</u>

A firm's strategy formulation is developed at several levels; first business level strategy addresses the issue. Of how to compete in a given business to attain competitive advantage, strategies are formulated after

Probing the following questions?

ADAPTING TO CHANGE – KEY STRATEGIC MANAGEMENT QUESTIONS

- *What kind of business should we become?*

- *Are we in the right fields?*
- *Should we reshape our business?*
- *What new competitors are entering our industry?*
- *What strategies should we pursue?*
- *How are our customers changing?*

The firm must determine the best method to develop international strategies as it ventures beyond its national boundaries, managers must formulate effective entrepreneurial initiatives to succeed in highly competitive and dynamic environment.

Step 7 -Strategy implementation:

Sound strategy is of no value if they are not properly implemented. Strategy implementation involves ensuring proper strategic control and organizational designs, which include

establishing effective means to coordinate and integrate activities within the firm as well as with its suppliers, customers, and alliance partners, Leadership plays a central role, including ensuring that the organization is committed to excellence and ethical behavior. It also promotes learning and continuous improvement and acts entrepreneurially in creating and taking advantage of new opportunities.

Step 8: Strategy evaluation and control:

Firms must exercise two types of strategic control. First informational control requires that organizations continually monitor and scan the environment and responds to threats and opportunities. Second, behavioral control involves the proper balance of rewards and incentives as well as cultures and boundaries. Successful firms practice effective corporate governance. They must create mechanisms to ensure that the actions of the managers are consistent with the interests of the owners of the firms. These include an effective board of directors, actively engaged shareholders and proper managerial rewards and incentive systems, various external mechanisms such as market of corporate control, auditors, banks, analysts, and the financial press often help to ensure good governance.

Strategic decision making:

Management is the process of decision making. All decisions are important as one decisions leads to another decision which has major or minor effect on the organizations. Appropriate decisions making is basic and fundamental for the survival and growth of the firms.

Proper analysis, conceptual ability, comprehensive thinking, far-sightedness, should be some abilities for strategic decision making; It is a major choice of actions concerning allocation of resources and contribution to the achievement of organizations objectives.

Attributes of strategic decision making:

- It is fundamental, as it influences the entire or major part of the organizations.
- Strategic decisions contribute directly to the organizational goals. They have a long term impact.
- It has to consider various other alternatives to buffer against the volatile environment. All these alternatives impact the outcome, inputs and profitability

14

- Strategic decision are trade-offs between the costs and risks and time, competitive vulnerability of the market. They are controversial in nature

- Difficulty in reconciling stakeholders' Needs.

Approaches to strategic decision making:

Since organizations are unique in their own way, the decision making styles varies among them. The differences may arise due to the extent of formalization of decisions, move from formalized and structured to informal and unstructured, process, managerial power relationships etc.

Henry Mintzberg has identified three different approaches of decisions making:

- Entrepreneurial approach: is followed by business held by families, who constantly searchfor opportunities that changing environment makes available, decisions making is more or less centralized, where rich experience and past sound judgment plays a vital role in making the head as competent authority to make decisions, they are both growth and expansions oriented. They keep the organizations adaptive to changing needs of business world.

- Adaptive approach:this approach is reactive rather than proactive and tries to collect andmix the variant factors influencing strategic decisions. It is more of problem solving which are encountered for survival in business, Decisions making is the hands of many people evolved in the process, and priority based decisions are taken into considerations.

- Planning approach:strategic decisions are based on socio-economic situations, purposes oforganizations, value of top management, external opportunities. Decision making is a comprehensive step of systematic and structured analysis of the environment effecting the organizations.

Pitfalls in strategic management:Strategic management is however a liability when thingsdo not fall in the right quadrant, even after a lot of thorough analysis, there are certain limitations which are to be taken into account before one is concluding strategic management is be always successful.

- It inflicts rigidity in the organizations: when there is no match in strategy formulation and implementation.

15

- Short-term focus of the organization: long terms changes will not be appreciated as today organizations focus in short term results,

- Ever changing, complex and dynamic environment:

- Review process is difficult and time consuming activity.

<u>Reasons for failure of Strategic Management</u>: There are many reasons why strategic plansfail, especially:
a.Failure to understand the customer

- Why do they buy
- Is there a real need for the product
- inadequate or incorrect marketing research

b.Inability to predict environmental reaction
o What will competitors do

- Fighting brands
- Price wars
- Will government intervene

c.Over-estimation of resource competence

- Can the staff, equipment, and processes handle the new strategy
- Failure to develop new employee and management skills

d.Failure to coordinate

- Reporting and control relationships not adequate
- Organizational structure not flexible enough

e.Failure to obtain senior management commitment

- Failure to get management involved right from the start
- Failure to obtain sufficient company resources to accomplish task

f.Failure to obtain employee commitment

- New strategy not well explained to employees
- No incentives given to workers to embrace the new strategy

g.Under-estimation of time requirements

- No critical path analysis done

h.Failure to follow the plan

- No follow through after initial planning
- No tracking of progress against plan
- No consequences for above

i.Failure to manage change
• Inadequate understanding of the internal resistance to change
• Lack of vision on the relationships between processes, technology and organization
j.Poor communications

- Insufficient information sharing among stakeholders
- Exclusion of stakeholders and delegates

Who are Strategic Managers?

There are two kinds of senior managers most directly responsible for strategy: Business managers and corporate managers. Business managers are in charge of individual business, In diversified, multi business firms, the executives in charge of individual business (electronic, semiconductors, serves) are business managers, these executives go by many designations like general manager, division manager, strategic business manager.

Corporate managers are responsible for portfolios of business, In multi-business firm the president or chairperson, are corporate manager, they oversee the subset of the firm's total portfolio of business.

Both these business and corporate managers play pivotal roles in the strategic management process, they are key people who bring all other assets into play when competing with other firms. They also represent the highest level of authority within the firm or subunit. As a result, they exert enormous influence over the company's capital expenditure to build new plants ore to acquire other companies, chart the future direction of the firm's growth and direct the firm's efforts towards emerging market opportunities. Top managers often serve as the

spokespersons for their firms when dealing with the media over such issues as breakthrough technologies, new products rollouts, or potential allegations against the company by shareholders, customers or communities. Thus top managers perform multiple tasks at the highest level of an organization and bear the highest responsibility for their firm's strategies and actions.

At the same time, customers, investors, employees and even the public at large depend on the judgment, experience and skills of these managers to compete both fairly and within the law. For the vast majority of companies in India, senior managers continue to work long hours formulating strategies and action plans that aim to satisfy their customers, rewards their investors, develop their employees, and foster a large sense of public trust. However business is not immune from scandalous activities that can mar the reputation of entire industries for an extended period.

The strategic managers include:

- Board of directors.
- Chief executive officer/managing director.
- Entrepreneur.
- SBU level managers.
- Senior managers.
- Middle-level managers.
- Lower level manager

Roles of strategic manager a. **Interpersonal Roles:**

- Figure Head.
- Leader.
- Liaison

b.**Informational Role:**

18

- Monitor.
- Disseminator.
- Spokesman.

c.**Decisional Roles:**

- Disturbance Handler.
- Intrepreneur.
- Resources Allocator.
- Negotiator.

Strategic Management Responsibilities:

- Establishing the Mission:The strategist decides on the business engagement and guidancefor continuous growth. A mission is usually enduring and timeless.

- Formulating a Company Philosophy:Establishing the beliefs, values, attitudes andunwritten guide lines.

- **Setting Objectives:** deciding on achievement targets within a defined time range.Objectives help in making operational plans for carrying out strategy.

- Developing strategy: developing concepts, ideas and plans for achieving objectivessuccessfully and meeting and beating competition.

- Planning the organizational structure: developing the plan of the organization and theactivities that help people work to perform activities in accordance.

- Providing Personnel: recruiting, selection and developing people to fill the positions in theorganization.

- Establishing Procedures and facilities: Providing plant, equipment. Determining andprescribing how all the activities are carried out.

- Providing capital: making sure the business has the money, and credit needed for workingcapital and physical facilities.

- Establishing Management programme and operational plans: Developing programmes,and plans governing activities and the use of resources that carried out in accordance with established strategy, policies, procedures and standards will enable people to achieve particular objective.

19

- Providing control information: providing facts and figures to help people follow strategy,policies, procedures and programme to keep alert for the workforce. It also measures overall company performance against plans and standards.

- Activating people: Commanding and motivating people to act in accordance withphilosophy, policies, procedures and standards in carrying out the Plans of the company.

Conclusion:

An organization strategy must be appropriate for its resources, environment, circumstances and core objectives. The process involves matching the company's strategic advantage to business environment the organization faces.

One objective of overall corporate stage is to put the organization into a position to carry out its mission effectively and efficiently. A good corporate strategy should integrate the organizational goals, policies and action sequence (tactics) into a cohesive whole, and must be based on business realities. Business enterprise may fail despite excellent strategy because the world changes in a way they fail to understand. Strategy must connect with vision,

Purpose and likely future trends.

Strategic Competency in Action:Competing in global Markets: Philips Electronics:

Philips Electronics is one of the world's biggest producers of medical equipment, consumer electronics, semi-conductors, flat screen technologies, and home appliances. A European company with a very product tradition of innovation, Philips has consistently led the world in developing many important technologies. For example, it helped pioneer medical X-ray technology, the audio-cassette, the electric shaver, and today current compact discs technology. Yet for all its creative flair in the labs, Philips has struggled to compete with the likes of Matsushita, Sony and Samsung in the marketplace.

A big factor behind Philip' outstanding record of innovation is that the company has long encouraged scientific research and big projects that yield potentially big payoffs. While cultivating innovations, Philips has traditionally marketed its products in different parts of the world separately. Although Philips originated in the Netherlands, the company has historically looked to larger markets in the US, Latin America, Asia and the rest of Europe for much of its

20

growth. Philips was one of the first companies to formulate and implement a worldwide strategy that witnessed the steady growth and profitability of local operations. Many of Philips innovations over time came from large labs located throughout the US, Europe, Australia and Canada. Over time, Philips relied heavily on its regional affiliated to manufacture many of its leading-edge products for sale in national and more local markets.

The innovation driven strategy worked for Philips for many decades. Japanese rivals such as Matsushita Electric, Sony, JVC, and Toshiba began producing consumer electronics and other high technology products at lower unit costs. Unlike Philips, Japanese firms were able to construct large factories that were ultra efficient. They were able to overtake Philips' market position in many markets. Philips also faced competition, and difficulties building up a well-recognized brand name with global reach.

Philips attempted to restructure its operations to compete more effectively with these rivals over the past two decades. Its current CEO Gerard Kleisterlee is overseeing a major reorganizations of Philips that seeks to combine disparate operations and organizational practices into a cohesive system. Kleisterlee wants Phillips traditionally separate business units to communicate and to coordinate their activities to achieve significant cost savings and to deliver leading edge products to market faster. At the same time, the company has decided to allocate more resources to high growth opportunities in its core medical, electronics, and flat screen business.

In addition, Philips has formed a wide array of technologies sharing relation ships with companies throughout the US and Far East. With LG group Philips formed a separate company known as LG Philips of LCD screens that are found in flat screen TVs and Cell phones and digital cameras. Philips teamed with Chinese maker of medical equipment known as Neusoft, will produce medical imaging equipment for use in china. In the filed of advanced integrated circuits, Philips joined with Taiwan Semiconductor company to co design and co-produce leading edge chips that will power next generation applicants and consumer electronics. It is also working with Samsung Electronic to create "electronic wallet", it has also an ambition to be an important supplier of new digital technologies for future home entertainment centers.

21

Philips strategic transition is designed to compete more effectively in an increasingly connected global marketplace. However the process of chaining Philips organizational practices represents a long term ongoing effort that has already helped the company become more profitable and faster moving.

Summary:

- Strategy is a powerful concept designed to help firm gain a competitive advantage over rivals. It involves two key choices, the customers a firm will serve and the competences and strengths it will develop to serve customers effectively.
- A firm's choices must reflect its strength and weakness relative to rivals and the opportunities and threats presented by its external environment. Analysis of these four elements is refereed as SWOT analysis.
- All firms must deal with the strategic imperatives facing them according to their own individual situations.
- The management process designed to satisfy strategic imperatives for building competitive advantage is called strategic management process. It consists of four major steps: analysis, formulation, implementation, and evaluation.
- Because strategic choices involve large finances, have long term impact on an organization and generate considerable controversy among organizational members, top and senior managers generally play a primary role in determining such decisions.
- Executives most directly responsible for strategic decisions are business managers and corporate managers. A business manager is in charge of an entire business and corporate managers, oversees a portfolio of business.

Important Questions:

- Define Strategic management? Discuss its importance and relevance in today's volatile environment?
- Who is a strategist? What the role and responsibilities he plays?

22

- What is strategic management process? Explain in detail the steps involved?
- What is strategic decision making? What is the importance of decision making?
- What are reasons for strategic decision failure? Give relevant examples.

23

CHAPTER TWO

Strategy Formulation

Strategy Formulation

Strategy Formulation

- Definition of Strategy Formulation
- Developing Strategic Vision & Mission for a Company
- Business Policies, Objectives, Goals.
- Balance Score card.
- Strategic Intent- hierchy
- Merging Strategic Vision, Objectives, strategy to Strategic Plan.

Strategy Formulation: An Overview

The corporate world is in the process of a global transformation. Mergers, acquisitions, outsourcing and downsizing are becoming common word everywhere. Privatization is allowing free enterprise to take on functions that previously were the domain of government. International boundaries are fading in importance as businesses take on a more global perspective and the technology of information age is telescoping the time it takes to communicate and make decision. Strategic management takes a panoramic view of this changing corporate terrain and attempts to show how large and small firms can be more effective and efficient not only in today's world but tomorrow as well.

Strategic management is the set of managerial decisions and action that determines the way for the long-range performance of the company. It includes environmental scanning, strategy formulation, strategy implementation, evaluation and control. It emphasizes the monitoring and evaluation of external opportunities and threats in light of corporation's strength and weakness.

Business policy has a general management orientation and tends primarily to look inward with its concern for properly integrating the corporations many functional activities. But strategic management as a field of study integrates the business policy with the environmental opportunities and threats. Therefore strategic management has tended to replace business policy as the preferred name of the field.

Module 2 -Strategy Formulation

Strategy formulation:

Strategy formulation is the development of long range plans for the effective management of environmental opportunities and threats in light of corporate strengths and weaknesses. It includes defining the corporate mission, specifying achievable objectives, developing strategies and setting policy guidelines. It begins with situational analysis. The simplest way is to analyze through is SWOT analysis. This is the method to analyze the strengths and weakness in order to utilize the threat and to overcome the threat. SWOT is the acronym for Strength, Weakness, Opportunities and Threats. The TOWS matrix illustrates how the external opportunities and threats facing a particular corporation can be matched with that company's internal strengths and weaknesses to result in four sets of possible strategic alternatives.

How Are Vision & Mission Statements Used to Set the Strategic Direction?

Mission Statement: A mission statement is a statement of the purpose of a company or organization. The mission statement should guide the actions of the organization, spell out its overall goal, provide a path, and guide decision-making. It provides "the framework or context within which the company's strategies are formulated.

Effective mission statements commonly clarify the organization's purpose.

Commercial mission statements often include the following information:

• Purpose and aim(s) of the organization

• The organization's primary stakeholders: clients/customers, shareholders, congregation, etc.

• How the organization provides value to these stakeholders, for example by offering specific types of products and/or services.

• Examples of effective Mission statements include:

• Erie Insurance: "To provide our policyholders with as near perfect protection, as near perfect service as is humanly possible and to do so at the lowest possible cost."

• Nature Air: "To offer travelers a reliable, innovative and fun airline to travel in Central America."

• Nissan: "Nissan provides unique and innovative automotive products and services that deliver superior, measurable values to all stakeholders in alliance with Renault."

Importance of Mission Statement

? It helps in unity of direction among individuals.

? It serves as a focal point for individuals to identify with the organization's Purpose and direction

? It facilitates the translation of objectives into tasks assigned to responsible person within organization.

? It specifies organizational Purpose.

Characteristics of Mission Statement: In order to be effective, a mission statement should possess the following seven characteristics.

1. It should be feasible A mission should always aim high but it should not be an impossible statement. It should be realistic and achievable its followers must find it to be credible. But feasibility depends on the resources available to work towards a mission. In the sixties, the US National Aeronautics and Space Administration (NASA) had a mission to land on the moon. It was a feasible mission that was ultimately realized.

2. It should be precise. A mission statement should not be so narrow as to restrict the organization's activities nor should it be too broad to make itself meaningless. For instance, 'Manufacturing bicycles' is a narrow mission statement since it severely limits the organization's activities, while mobility business' is too broad a term, as it does not define the reasonable contour within which the organization could operate.

3. It should be clear. A mission should be clear enough to lead to action. It should not be a high sounding set of platitudes meant for publicity purposes. Many organizations do adopt such statements but probably they do so for emphasizing their identity and character. For example, Asian Paints stresses leadership through excellence', while India Today see itself as 'the complete news magazine'. The Administrative Staff

Module 2 -Strategy Formulation

College of India considers itself as 'the college for practicing managers' and Bajaj Auto believes in 'Providing, value for money, for years'. To be useful, a mission statement should be clear enough to lead to action. The ITC's stated corporate philosophy of aligning its organizational activities with national priorities helps it in choosing areas for diversification like the hotel, paper and agro industry.

4. It should be motivating. A mission statement should be motivating for members of the organization and of society, and they should feel it worthwhile working for such an organization or being its customers. A bank, which lays great emphasis on customer service, is likely to motivate its employees to serve its customers well and to attract clients. Customer service, therefore is an important purpose for a banking institution.

5. It should be distinctive. A mission statement, which is indiscriminate, is likely to have little impact. If all scooter manufacturers defined their mission in a similar fashion, there would not be much of a difference among them. But if one defines it as providing scooters that would provide 'value for money, for years' it will create an important distinction in the public mind.

6. It should indicate major components of strategy. A mission statement along with the organizational purpose should indicate the major components of the strategy to be adopted. The chief executive of Indal expressed his intentions by saying that his company "begins its fifth decade of committed entrepreneurship with the promise of a highly diversified company retaining aluminum as its mainline business, but with an active presence in the chemical, electronics and industrial equipment business". This statement indicates that the company is likely to follow a combination of stability, growth and diversification strategies in the future.

7. It should indicate how objectives are to be accomplished. Besides indicating the broad strategies to be adopted a mission statement should also provide clues regarding the manner in which the objectives are to be accomplished. The Centre for Development of Telematics (CDOT) had set its first three years mission (1984-87) as developing, designing, and engineering a large digital exchange suitable for Indian

Module 2 -Strategy Formulation

conditions and its second mission (1987-90) as developing the technological prerequisites for an integrated systems digital network of the future. These mission statements specially deal with the objectives to be achieved within a given time period.

Components of Mission statement

It includes the following components

? Basic product or service

? Principal Technology

? Customers

? Concern for survival, growth & Profitability

? Company self concept

? Concern for employees

? Concern for Public Image

Example: McDonald: "To offer the customer fast food Prepared in the same high quality worldwide, tasty and reasonably priced, delivered in a consistent low key décor and friendly manner"

Meaning and Definition of vision Statement

? "Vision is a clear mental picture of a future goal created jointly by a group for the benefit of other people, which is capable of inspiring and motivating those whose support is necessary for its achievement."

? Vision is " an ambition about the future, articulated today, it is a process of managing the present from a stretching view of the future"

Nature of vision

? It represents animating dream about the future.

? Powerful motivator to action

? It captures both minds and heart of people.

Example: Hindustan Lever: Our vision is to meet the everyday needs of people everywhere.

Microsoft: Empower people through great software any time, any place and on any device

Definition:

A vision statement is sometimes called a picture of your company in the future but it's so much more than that. Your vision statement is your inspiration, the framework for all your strategic planning.

A vision statement may apply to an entire company or to a single division of that company. Whether for all or part of an organization, the vision statement answers the question, "Where do we want to go?"

Characteristics of a Good Vision Statement: The Characteristics of a Good Vision statement as follows:

1. Brevity: A good vision statement is succinct, which makes it easy for managers and leaders to communicate and employees to remember. Vision statements are less effective when they are too short (such as a one-sentence vision statement) or too long (such as a two or three page vision statement). But exactly how long should it be? The average vision statement is about 35 words, or two to three Sentences. This length seems to be about right for effectively communicating the vision statement to Employees. It is long enough to clearly describe the vision but not so long as to be difficult to remember.

2. Clarity: A vision should unite the organization and provide a stable, transcendent goal. The vision should avoid using jargon and buzz words and should use understandable terminology. Writing concise a sentence is another way of clarifying a vision statement.

3. Abstract and Challenging: An effective vision statement sets an abstract yet challenging goal. The goal should not be stated too concretely (e.g., "to build a new building") but rather at a higher level of abstraction (e.g., "to create beautiful living

spaces"). This allows it to be relevant to all employees, thus permitting it to guide their daily actions and decisions. Abstractness also provides for flexibility. The following vision statement does a good job at communicating an abstract, challenging goal in a manner that is both clear and succinct:

Our business vision is to make interior environments more beautiful through the valuable, careful, and efficient production of architectural millwork, thereby providing an enriched quality of life to all who view and use our work.

4. States the Organization's Purpose: A vision should state a general idea of why the organization exists but should avoid including overly general statements such as to "develop new markets" or "to be the best". These types of vision statements will not provide effective guidance to employees who are responsible for developing ideas for new products/services or addressing new competitors. An effective vision statement should describe what the organization intends to achieve. The statement of purpose can include the organization's current or desired products or services, its markets (industry, sub-industries, geographic locations, or customers) in which it intends to offer those products and services, and the impact that its products and services are intended to have.

5. Future Focused: Good vision statements are long-term, describing the organization's desired end-state well into the future. Effective vision statements often describe on-going actions in which the organization will engage. The following is an example of a future-oriented vision statement: Our goal is to achieve 100% customer satisfaction for every product that we sell. We will be relentless in the pursuit of that goal and will never vary from the principles of customer satisfaction: Quality, Value, and Company Image.

6. Sets a Desirable Goal: A good vision statement inspires followers by setting a desirable goal. It may emphasize: Fundamental values We will nurture long-term partnerships with employees, customers, and suppliers built on consideration, trust, open communications, integrity, and professionalism. A collective identity We will strive to be the professional team of choice, offering quality engineering and technical services focused on customer satisfaction. We will provide a quality product, on time and within budget, which will exceed our customers' expectations.

The organization's uniqueness (its employees, customers, resources, etc.) We will be known for the striking beauty of veneer cabinets that we will sell to the nation's most famous hotels.

Employees' worth and efficacy we are determined to become a university whose people take pride in their accomplishments and their future potential.

7. Matches the Organization's Success Measures:

• Achievement we will make production as efficient as possible while keeping our commitment to quality.

• Affiliation we will strive to always be courteous in dealing with our neighbors, visitors and customers.

• Importance of Vision and Mission Statement : The importance of vision and mission statements to effective strategic management is well documented in the literature, although research results are mixed. Rarick and Vition found that firms with a formalized mission statement have twice the aerate return on shareholders' equity than those firms without a formalized mission statement have, Bart and Baetz found a positive relationship between mission statements and organizational performance; Business Week reports that firms using mission statements have a 30 percent higher return on certain financial measures than those without such statements; however, some studies have found that having a mission statement does not directly contribute positively to financial performance. The extent of manager and employee involvement in developing vision and mission statements can make a difference in business success. This post provides guidelines for developing these important documents. In actual practice, wide variations exist in the nature, composition, and use of both vision and mission statements. King and Cleland recommend that organizations carefully develop a written mission statement for the following reasons.

1. To ensure unanimity of purpose within the organization
2. To provide a basis, or standard, for allocating organizational resources
3. To establish a general tone or organizational climate
4. To serve as a focal point for individuals to identify with the organization's purpose and direction, and to deter those who cannot from participating further in the organization's activities

Module 2 -Strategy Formulation

5. To facilitate the translation of objectives into a work structure involving the assignment of tasks to responsible elements within the organization
6. To specify organizational purposes and then to translate these purposes into objectives in such a way that cost, time, and performance parameters can be assessed and controlled.

Benefits of Vision Statement: The process and outcomes of visioning may seem vague and superfluous. The long-term benefits are substantial, however. Visioning:

• Breaks you out of boundary thinking.
• Provides continuity and avoids the stutter effect of planning fits and starts.
• Identifies direction and purpose.
• Alerts stakeholders to needed change.

- Promotes interest and commitment.
- Promotes laser-like focus.
- Encourages openness to unique and creative solutions.
- Encourages and builds confidence.
- Builds loyalty through involvement (ownership).
- Results in efficiency and productivity.

Distinguish between vision and mission
Vision Statement Mission Statement
? A mental image of possible and ? Enduring statement of Philosophy
desirable future state of organization ? The purpose or reason of firms
? A dream existence
? Broad ? More specific than vision
? Answers the question "what we want ? Answers the question "What is our
to become? Business".
9

Module 2 -Strategy Formulation

Definition Business Policy

- Business policy may be defined as "Specific guidelines to managerial action and decision in the implementation of strategy".
- "A policy is a statement or a commonly accepted understanding of decision making criteria or formula prepared or evolved to achieve efficiency in operation by making relevant decision".

Importance of Business policies:

Sound business policies are capable of making an organization more power charged to attain certain benefits to the organization.

1. Policies provide a definite framework within which decisions are taken by subordinates.
2. It helps to solve business problems.
3. Policies provide stability in administration.
4. Paves ways to well-knit coordination
5. Policies help in enhancing managerial skill.
6. Optimum utilization of human and material resources is possible
7. Policies serve as yardstick for measuring performances.
8. Policies help in creating positive good-will and image building.

Features of Business Policy

- An effective business policy must have following features-
- Specific- Policy should be specific/definite. If it is uncertain, then the implementation will become difficult.
- Clear- Policy must be unambiguous. It should avoid use of jargons and connotations. There should be no misunderstandings in following the policy.
- Reliable/Uniform- Policy must be uniform enough so that it can be efficiently followed by the subordinates.
- Appropriate- Policy should be appropriate to the present organizational goal.
- Simple- A policy should be simple and easily understood by all in the organization.

Module 2 -Strategy Formulation

• Flexible- Policy should be flexible in operation/application. This does not imply that a policy should be altered always, but it should be wide in scope so as to ensure that the line managers use them in repetitive/routine scenarios.

• Stable- Policy should be stable else it will lead to indecisiveness and uncertainty in minds of those who look into it for guidance.

Difference between Policy and Strategy

• The term "policy" should not be considered as synonymous to the term "strategy". The difference between policy and strategy can be summarized as follows-

• Policy is a blueprint of the organizational activities which are repetitive/routine in nature. While strategy is concerned with those organizational decisions which have not been dealt/faced before in same form.

• Policy formulation is responsibility of top level management. While strategy formulation is basically done by middle level management.

• Policy deals with routine/daily activities essential for effective and efficient running of an organization. While strategy deals with strategic decisions.

• Policy is concerned with both thought and actions. While strategy is concerned mostly with action.

• A policy is what is, or what is not done. While a strategy is the methodology used to achieve a target as prescribed by a policy.

Objectives of Policies:

Policies are formulated to achieve long-term goals and objectives of the organization:

1. Knowledge sharing and knowledge generation.
2. Skill creation
3. Attitudinal change to cope with business situation.

Module 2 -Strategy Formulation

Essentials of Business policy:

1. Objective based.
2. Clarity and Simplicity.
3. Written form.
4. Stable yet flexible.
5. Complementary /supplementary.
6. Comprehensive
7. Consistency
8. Pro-ethical
9. Individualistic.

Business policies are influenced by the following factors:

1. Vision, goals, and objectives of the enterprise.
2. Managerial structure/philosophy/attitude of the management.
3. Resources at its disposal.
4. Social and ethical values at the top management.
5. Economic, industrial, fiscal and commercial policy of the government.
6. Policies of sister concern/ business associates.
7. Public opinion

Classification of Business Policies

Policies are broadly classified into:

Major policies: relate to the organizational level objectives and procedures, control covering the entire organization.

Major policies relate to capital structure, organizational structure, pricing structure, personnel approaches to merger, acquisition, diversification, R&D and technology. These policies are framed by Top Management with the shareholders.

Minor Policies: Minor policies are outgrowth of major policies. They are supportive policies which smoothens the functions of the organization by enhancing efficiency level. They cover functional areas of the organization.

Module 2 -Strategy Formulation

Policies cover various areas of management:

a) Top Management policies.
b) Middle management policies
c) Lower level policies.
d) Functional policies

i) Marketing and sales policies: These policies relate to matters like display, advertising, Salesmanship. Product mix, market mix, establishing sales volume and expenditure, pricing, selection of channels of distribution.

ii) Financial policies. The entire success of business depends upon financial policies which deals with capital requirement, methods of rising funds, deciding on capital structure, credit terms, profit policy and tax provisions.

iii) Personnel policies.: Human resources policies deals with human resource utilization, its recruitment, and selection, training of employees, promotion and transfer, issues relating to compensation to employees.

iv) Production policies: They are concerned with the type of product produced, the selection of technology, equipment and process, selection, location, site and layout.

v) Contingency policies: In the course of business unexpected happenings may occur. Such events might adversely effect the smooth functioning of the business. To meet such unforeseen situations, contingency policies are formulated to enable to meet the situation whenever they arise.

Business policies involve steps like:

1. Formulation: The main object of generating the policy is to have smooth working in the business organization. After detail analysis of internal and external environment must be taken into consideration before formulating policies.

2. Interpretation: converting the policies into activities to be followed and announcement or making the subject-matter aware among the employees.

3. Acceptance: When policies are formulated it is advisable to get the draft of the
policies statement approved by those who are supposed to apply it in the interest of the

Module 2 -Strategy Formulation

4. Implementation: This step indicates putting it into practice as when any problem or critical situation arises.

5. Feedback and review: policy implemented should take place in conformity with the basic principles, rules and regulation set by the policy makers.

Objectives: Objective is concrete goals that the organization seeks to reach, for example an earnings growth target. The objective must be achievable and challenging, and measurable so that the company can monitor its progress and make corrections as needed.

- Objectives are formulated to accomplish Organization Mission.
- Objectives can be defined as "The long term results that an organization seeks to achieve in pursuing its basic mission".

Example: Objectives of Tesco Company

- Offering customers the best value for money and the most competitive prices.

• Meeting the needs of customers by constantly seeking, and acting on, their opinions regarding innovation, product quality, choice, store facilities and service.

Importance of Objectives

• Objectives indicate the purpose and aims of organisation.
• Objectives provide directions for the functioning of an organisation.
• It helps to adjust itself to the existing environment.
• Helps in attaining employee's coordination and therefore reduce conflicts.
• Helps in control and assessment of organisation performance.

Features of Good Objectives

• Objectives should be understandable.
• Objectives should be related to the time frame.

ictly for Private Circulation JU-CMS Lakshman K Page 14

Module 2 -Strategy Formulation

• Objectives should be specific
• Objective should be realistic.
• Measurability.
• Flexibility.
• Definition of Goals

"An objective or desired outcome; the end-point you want to reach."

Essentials of effective Goals

• Goals should be SMART
• Goals should be Specific
• Goals should be Measurable
• Goals should be Achievable
• Goals should be Realistic
• Goals should be Time bound.

Balanced Scorecard

The Balanced Scorecard is a strategic planning and management system used to align business activities to the vision and strategy of the organization by monitoring performance against strategic goals.

Balanced Scorecard Concept

• Was first published in 1992 by Kaplan and Norton, a book followed in 1996.
• Traditional performance measurements that only focus on external accounting data are obsolete.
• The approach is to provide 'balance' to the financial perspective.

Module 2 -Strategy Formulation

• Balances financial and non-financial measures: Balance Score card Method is used to balance the Financial and non financial measures of the company.
• Balances short and long-term measures: Balance Score Card Method is also used both short and long term measures of the company. This can be used for routine activities of the firm and also for achieving long term Objective.
• Balances performance drivers (leading indicators) with outcome measures (lagging indicators)
• Should contain just enough data to give a complete picture of organizational performance... and no more.
• Leads to strategic focus and organizational alignment.

Reasons for Using Balance Score card

- Improve organizational performance by measuring what matters
- Increase focus on strategy and results
- Align organization strategy with workers on a day-to-day basis
- Focus on the drivers key to future performance
- Improve communication of the organization's Vision and Strategy
- Prioritize Projects / Initiatives.

Balanced Scorecard Basics: 4 Original Business Perspectives

- The Balanced Scorecard model suggests that we view the organization from 4 perspectives
- Then Develop metrics, collect data and analyze it relative to each of these perspectives.

Module 2 -Strategy Formulation

Adapted from Robert S. Kaplan and David P. Norton, "Using the Balanced Scorecard as a Strategic Management System," Harvard Business Review (January-February 1996): 76.

Perspectives

The balanced scorecard suggests that we view the organization from four perspectives, and to develop metrics, collect data and analyze it relative to each of these perspectives:

The Learning & Growth Perspective

This perspective includes employee training and corporate cultural attitudes related to both individual and corporate self-improvement. In a knowledge-worker organization, people -- the only repository of knowledge -- are the main resource. In the current climate of rapid technological change, it is becoming necessary for knowledge workers to be in a continuous learning mode. Metrics can be put into place to guide managers in focusing training funds where they can help the most. In any case, learning and growth constitute the essential foundation for success of any knowledge-worker organization.

Kaplan and Norton emphasize that 'learning' is more than 'training'; it also includes things like mentors and tutors within the organization, as well as that ease of communication among workers that allows them to readily get help on a problem when it is needed. It also includes technological tools; what the Baldrige criteria call "high performance work systems."

The Business Process Perspective

This perspective refers to internal business processes. Metrics based on this perspective allow the managers to know how well their business is running, and whether its products and services conform to customer requirements (the mission). These metrics have to be carefully designed by those who know these processes most intimately; with our unique missions these are not something that can be developed by outside consultants.

Module 2 -Strategy Formulation

The Customer Perspective

Recent management philosophy has shown an increasing realization of the importance of customer focus and customer satisfaction in any business. These are leading indicators: if customers are not satisfied, they will eventually find other suppliers that will meet their needs. Poor performance from this perspective is thus a leading indicator of future decline, even though the current financial picture may look good.

In developing metrics for satisfaction, customers should be analyzed in terms of kinds of customers and the kinds of processes for which we are providing a product or service to those customer groups.

The Financial Perspective

Kaplan and Norton do not disregard the traditional need for financial data. Timely and accurate funding data will always be a priority, and managers will do whatever necessary to provide it. In fact, often there is more than enough handling and processing of financial data. With the implementation of a corporate database, it is hoped that more of the processing can be centralized and automated. But the point is that the current emphasis on financials leads to the "unbalanced" situation with regard to other perspectives. There is perhaps a need to include additional financial-related data, such as risk assessment and cost-benefit data, in this category.

Module 2 -Strategy Formulation

Example Of Balance score Card Method Of Oracle Company

Benefits of Balanced Scorecard

• Helps align key performance measures with strategy at all levels of an organization

• The methodology facilitates communication and understanding of business goals and strategies at all levels of an organization

• Strategic initiatives that follow "best practices" methodologies that cascade through the entire organization

• Transforms an organization's mission statement and strategic plan from a passive document into the "marching orders" for the organization on a daily basis.

• It enables executives to truly execute their strategies by identifying what should be done and measured.

Scorecard Potential Pitfalls & Criticisms

• Lack of a well Defined Strategy: The balanced scorecard relies on a well defined strategy and understanding of linkages between strategic objections and metrics. Without this foundation the implementation could fail.

• Too much focus on the lagging measures: Focusing on only the lagging measures may cause a lack of priority or opportunity for the leading measures.

Module 2 -Strategy Formulation

• Use of Generic Metrics: Don't just copy metrics from another firm. Identify the measures that apply to your strategy and competitive position.

• Self-serving managers: Managers whose goal is to achieve a desired result in order to obtain a bonus or other self reward.

Strategic Intent:

• Strategic intent is a high-level statement of the means by which your organization will achieve its vision. It is a statement of design for creating a desirable future (stated in present terms). Putting it simple, a strategic intent is your company's vision of what it wants to achieve in the long term.

• Strategic Intent has a hierarchy- vision, Mission and goals and objectives.

Attributes of Strategic Intent

• Sense of Direction: Strategic Intent implies a particular view about long term market or competitive position that an organisation hopes to build in future.

• Sense of Discovery: Strategic Intent is differential as each organisation differs from others. It implies a competitively unique point view about the future.

• Sense of Destiny: strategic Intent has an emotional edge to it. It is an end result that employees perceive as inherently worthwhile

SOME SAMPLE STRATEGIC INTENTS FORD Motor Company

Our Vision: to become the world's leading company for automotive products and services.

Our Mission: we are a global, diverse family with a proud heritage, passionately committed to providing outstanding products and services.

Our Values: We do the right thing for our people, our environment and our society, but
above all for our customers.

Module 2 -Strategy Formulation

Merging the Strategic Vision, Objective and Strategy into a Strategic Plan

- The Vision is the primary statement. Based on Vision statement, the Mission statement is formed.
- The Objectives of the Company helps to prepare Strategic plan in various areas like marketing, finance, production.
- Hence the genesis is Vision and Objectives of the Company helps to draw the Strategic Plan in different are as of the Organization & Business.
- The strategic plan projects a prescriptive model based on predictive environment which is a road map for execution.
- Strategic plan is translated into the operations planning.
- Any deviation required is to be directed by strategic plan which takes care of the corporate objective and factors commanding the change.

Model Question Paper

a. What is Strategic Formation?
b. What is Mission Statement? Explain the features of Mission Statement.
c. What is Vision Statement? Explain the features of Vision Statement.
d. Explain the importance of Mission statement.
e. Explain the various components of Mission statement
f. Explain the benefits of Vision statement
g. Differentiate between Mission and vision Statement.
h. Define Business Policy? Explain the features of Business Policy.
i. Differentiate between Policy and Strategy.
j. Explain the various classification of Business Policy.
k. Define objective? What is the various importances of Objectives.
l. Explain the various features of Good Objectives.

Module 2 -Strategy Formulation

m. What is Balance score card Method? Explain the concept of Balance score card Method.
n. Explain the various usage of Balance score card Method
o. Explain the various benefits and Limitation of Balance Scorecard method.
p. What is Strategic Intent? Explain the various attributes of Strategic Intent.
q. Explain Merging the Strategic Vision, Objective and Strategy into a Strategic Plan.

9 798885 215480

Printed by Libri Plureos GmbH in Hamburg,
Germany